VOL. LXII, NO. 24

METROPOLIS' GREATEST NEWSPAPER

FRIDAY, MARCH 3RD 2000

WHERE HAS HE GONE?

ED EARLIER THIS YEAR, WHERE IS HE AND WHY DID HE GO?

SUPERMAN
RETURNS™

LONDON, NEW YORK, MUNICH,
MELBOURNE, and DELHI

Created by Tall Tree Ltd
Editor Jon Richards
Designer Ed Simkins
For DK
Senior Designer and Brand Manager Rob Perry
Publishing Manager Simon Beecroft
Category Publisher Alex Allan
DTP Designer Hanna Ländin
Production Amy Bennett

First published in the UK in 2006 by
Dorling Kindersley Limited
80 Strand, London WC2R 0RL
A Penguin Company

06 07 08 10 9 8 7 6 5 4 3 2 1

A CIP catalogue for this book is available from the British Library.

ISBN-10 1-4053-1427-3
ISBN-13 9781405314275

Colour reproduction by Media Development and Printing Ltd., UK
Printed and bound in Italy by L.E.G.O.

SUPERMAN
RETURNS™

THE VISUAL GUIDE
DANIEL WALLACE
SUPERMAN CREATED BY JERRY SIEGEL AND JOE SHUSTER

CONTENTS

SUPERMAN FOR ALL SEASONS

Created by writer Jerry Siegel and artist Joe Shuster,
and first appearing in the June 1938 issue of *Action Comics* #1,
Superman has been thrilling comic book fans, newspaper readers,
radio show listeners, TV viewers, Broadway audiences, and millions
and millions of movie watchers for nearly 70 years, with no signs of
slowing down. Superman was not only the very first comic book super hero,
he is arguably the most loved, and one of the most widely known characters
created in any medium. Ask nearly anyone on any continent, and even if they've never
seen a Superman movie or read one of his comic books, they'll still know who he is.

 Superman Returns, directed by Bryan Singer, is the seventh major motion picture starring
the Man of Steel and is unquestionably the biggest Superman movie yet. This is a movie
about personal growth, about what it means to be Superman, and about what effect he has

on the people who care for him and on the rest of the world. More than any of the other movies, *Superman Returns*, starring actor Brandon Routh, is about the *man* even more than it is about the *Super*. That Superman is first and foremost a man even before he is a hero explains his enduring quality, and why his popularity continues long after many other gaudy comic-book heroes have been forgotten. We care about Superman because he represents the best in us. He stands for truth and for justice. He is the us we wish we could be.

This book, filled with hundreds of magnificent photos from the movie and incisive text by writer Daniel Wallace, lets us accompany him on his new adventure, one that takes him to his home planet Krypton and back again, digs deep into his mind as well as his heart, and hopefully will be the first of many, many more journeys to come.

Marv Wolfman | 22 March 2006 | Tarzana, California, USA

WHO IS SUPERMAN?

To the public, the Man of Steel appeared like a bolt from the blue – a square-jawed champion who possessed powers normally held by angels. He made his debut in Metropolis, rescuing *Daily Planet* reporter Lois Lane after her helicopter crashed into a rooftop. Lois gave this amazing stranger a name: Superman. Through Lois's newspaper articles, the public learned more about Superman. He came from a destroyed planet called Krypton. He could fly, withstand nearly any injury, and melt almost any substance with his heat vision. He believed in truth and justice. He never lied, although he kept some things secret, including his upbringing in Smallville, Kansas, and his alternate identity as Clark Kent. Superman thwarted the deranged Lex Luthor's plans for world domination, but then he vanished. It has now been five years since his disappearance, and people have adjusted to life without their beloved super hero. The world doesn't know that far beyond the solar system, Superman has made a long trek to the planet of his birth. Against all odds, he hopes that Krypton somehow survived and that his birth parents may still be alive. Only they can reveal to him where he truly belongs in the universe.

THE BIRTH OF SUPERMAN

Without his parents' knowledge, Clark tests the limits of his powers

LEAPING TALL BUILDINGS

Before he could fly, he jumped. Once Clark discovered the amazing strength of his Kryptonian legs, he'd spend all day practising vaulting from one corner of the farm to the other. But without the power of flight, Clark couldn't change direction in mid-air. As a result, landings were sometimes messy, and he'd return home covered in mud and straw.

The rural seclusion of Smallville was a huge advantage for the growing Superman. Not only did he receive the loving care of his adoptive parents, Jonathan and Martha Kent, but the isolated farm provided the perfect playground for a boy learning to control his superpowers. Strength, speed, and resistance to injury were his first abilities, present from the moment the three-year-old Clark emerged from the craft that brought him to Earth. When Clark entered his early teens, he learned he could fly, and soon he achieved mastery over X-ray vision and heat vision. Jonathan Kent advised his son to watch his strength, keeping Clark away from high school sports where he might accidentally injure a team-mate. By the time Clark left Smallville, he knew when to use his powers, and when to keep them in check.

Experimenting with his superspeed, Clark races through the cornfields and leaves a miniature shockwave in his wake. No matter how fast he sprints, he never seems to get tired. With a running start, Clark has discovered that he can get more height and distance from his jump.

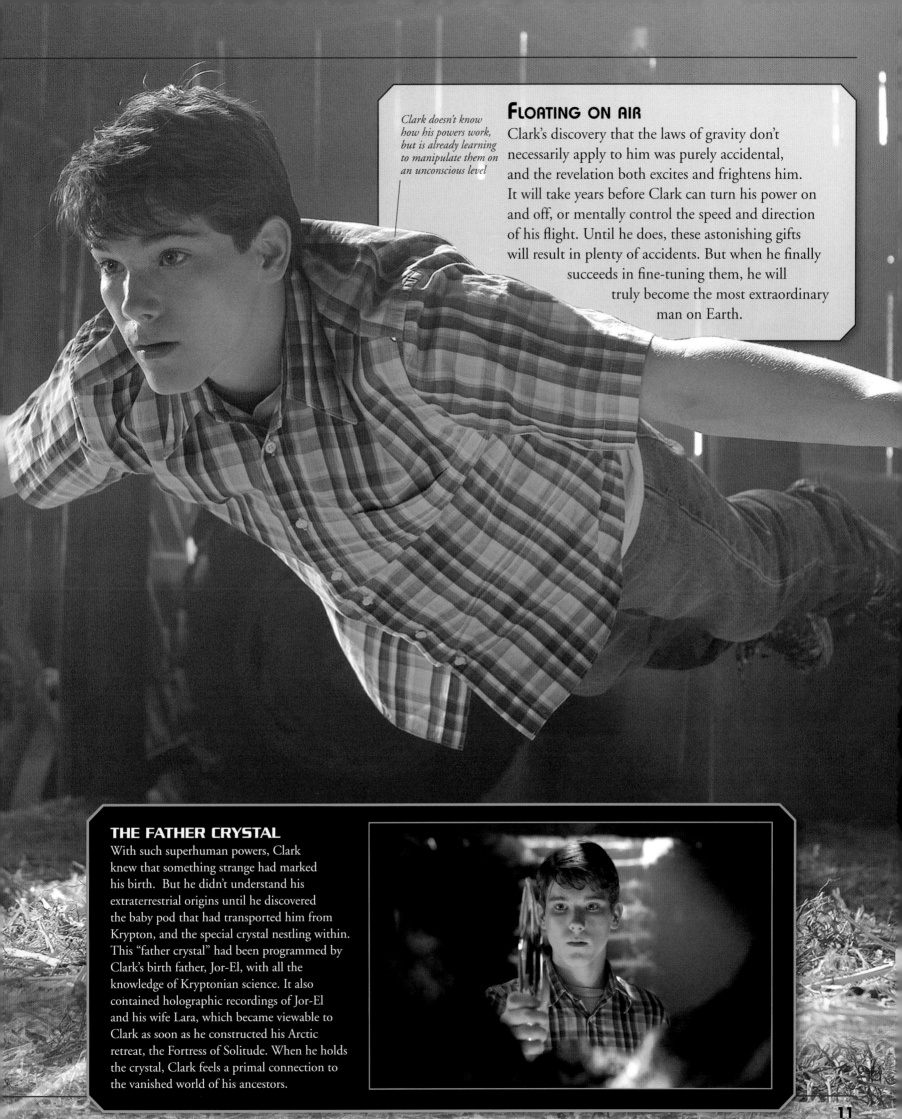

Clark doesn't know how his powers work, but is already learning to manipulate them on an unconscious level

FLOATING ON AIR

Clark's discovery that the laws of gravity don't necessarily apply to him was purely accidental, and the revelation both excites and frightens him. It will take years before Clark can turn his power on and off, or mentally control the speed and direction of his flight. Until he does, these astonishing gifts will result in plenty of accidents. But when he finally succeeds in fine-tuning them, he will truly become the most extraordinary man on Earth.

THE FATHER CRYSTAL

With such superhuman powers, Clark knew that something strange had marked his birth. But he didn't understand his extraterrestrial origins until he discovered the baby pod that had transported him from Krypton, and the special crystal nestling within. This "father crystal" had been programmed by Clark's birth father, Jor-El, with all the knowledge of Kryptonian science. It also contained holographic recordings of Jor-El and his wife Lara, which became viewable to Clark as soon as he constructed his Arctic retreat, the Fortress of Solitude. When he holds the crystal, Clark feels a primal connection to the vanished world of his ancestors.

WHERE HAS HE GONE?

Superman made no announcement about his journey to Krypton. The day after he saved Metropolis from a meteor shower, he simply disappeared – telling only Martha Kent of his destination and leaving Earth aboard a Kryptonian vessel. Millions of fans could only speculate about the super hero's whereabouts, worrying what would become of Metropolis without the Man of Steel. Believing that Krypton's star had not exploded and that the planet's inhabitants might still be alive, Superman embarked on a perilous journey into the farthest reaches of outer space. His absence was the perfect opportunity for criminal mastermind Lex Luthor to plot revenge against the Man of Steel.

"Where Has He Gone?" asked the *Daily Planet*, in a front-page headline published a year after Superman's disappearance. Such stories became less frequent over the next four years, as people became resigned to the fact that the Man of Steel had seemingly vanished for ever.

Data recorded by NASA's Cassini-Huygens satellite from a vantage point near Saturn suggested that Krypton's star did not suffer the catastrophe that Jor-El had feared. The possibility that his birth parents, not to mention his entire civilization, could still be alive proved an irresistible lure for Superman.

SCOOP!

The Daily Planet dates back to the late 1700s. But it was at the beginning of the 20th century, as it chronicled the industrial age, the space age, and the information age under a succession of cut-throat publishers that the newspaper hit its stride. Through the *Daily Planet*, news of World War II and the race to the moon was delivered to Metropolitans from newsstands. The newspaper's use of oversized photos and screaming type has led some to call it sensationalist, but even critics admit that the Planet's standard of investigative journalism is unmatched.

Reflecting Metropolis's forward-looking approach, the Daily Planet *has long been a supporter of the space program*

SUPER SELLER

When the Man of Steel made his Metropolis debut, he pushed every other story off the front page. Thanks to a romance between Superman and reporter Lois Lane, the Planet became a must-read for fans hungry for the latest Superman news. But not even editor-in-chief Perry White knew the true reason for the Planet's scoops — Superman worked at the newspaper, under the identity of Clark Kent.

The Planet was an early advocate for America's entry into World War II

FRONT PAGE NEWS

After Superman's disappearance, the *Daily Planet* speculated about his whereabouts and lamented the alarming rise in the city's crime rate. In time, any mention of Superman became less and less frequent, until Lois Lane published a story that urged the world to forget about its so-called saviour. Superman's sudden return electrifies the public and delights Perry White, who predicts that the newspaper will soon be printing many sellout editions.

The Daily Planet *went back to press several times to meet demand for this edition*

Daily Planet

DAILY PLANET

METROPOLIS' GREATEST NEWSPAPER

35 CENTS

THE PLANET'S EXCHANGE RATES

Austria.........12 S.	Kenya.........Shs. 6.00	
Belgium.........20 B.Fr.	Lebanon.........£ 2.00	
Denmark.........3.50 D.Kr.	Luxembourg.........20 L.Fr.	
Eire.........16 P.	Netherlands.........1.50 Flor	
Finland.........2.50 F.	Nigeria.........60 N.	
France.........2.50 B.Fr.	Norway.........3 N.Kr.	
Germany.........2.20 F.	Portugal.........15 Esc.	
Great Britain.........15 P.	Spain.........30 Ptas.	
Greece.........18 Drs.	Sweden.........2.50 S.Kr.	
India.........Rs.6	Switzerland.........1.70 S.Fr.	
Iran.........40 Rials	Turkey.........T.£ 8	
Italy.........400 Lire	Yugoslavia.........15 D.	
Israel.........I.£ 5.00	Zamanda.........15 Q.	

THE PLANET'S WEATHER AT A GLANCE

METROPOLIS: Monday, sunny with clear skies and low humidity. Temp. 88-89. Tuesday, cloudy with possible showers. WASHINGTON: Monday, cloudy with possible showers. Temp. 89-90. Tuesday cloudy with possible showers. Temp. 87-88. LONDON: Monday, clear. Temp. 83-84. Tuesday, variable. Temp. 83-84.

ADDITIONAL WEATHER - B12

THURSDAY SEPTEMBER, 28TH 2006

VOL. LXII, NO. 24

THE MAN OF STEEL IS BACK!

SUPERMAN APPEARS FROM NOWHERE TO SAVE SHUTTLE FROM DESTRUCTION

A mysterious black-out caused the much publicized Genesis Mission to malfunction. Amazingly Superman appeared from nowhere to save the day.

Lois Lane

The heroic return of Superman, after an absence of 6 long years, was witnessed today by thousands of stunned sporting fans attending the play-off match between the Miami Ravens and the Washington Fins at the stadium. Witnesses say Superman managed to stop the wingless fuselage of a Boeing 777 plummeting to earth, amazingly, as it reached the legendary stadium's home plate. The caped wonder then gently laid the aircraft on the field and all the passenger and crew members disembarked shocked and shaken, but unharmed.

Man of Steel returns to save thousands from certain death at the baseball stadium...

This same fuselage was to be the launch pad of the much anticipated Genesis Mission, a combined US Air Force and Virgin Galactic project; the first of a new generation of versatile, reusable space craft. This was to be the beginning of a new space program that would eventually establish Virgin Galactic as a leader in commercial space travel.

The highly anticipated Genesis Mission, reported to have been more than US$900 million dollars over budget on it's recent completion, was to be launched from the fuselage of the 777 whilst in flight at 40,000 feet. The first dual craft launch of an orbital shuttle, the new space craft uses on board "orbital insertion boost-

it into space. The previous shuttle needed twelve million pounds of G-thrust in its initial launch phase alone.

The near disaster occurred as the crew was preparing for booster ignition, [this is where the shuttle disengages from the 777 mid flight]. The origin of the power failure is not yet known, but US military sources indicate it originated

A mysterious power failure caused the launching sequence on Genesis to malfunction

somewhere near the harbour in central Metropolis.

The press junket on board the highly publicized Virgin Galactic shuttle launch involved 47 crew and passengers, including key US Air Force officials and a Virgin Galactic Team.

Both the US Air Force and Virgin Galactic blame the incident on a "mysterious power failure" which authorities believe caused a malfunction in the thruster sequence. This malfunction caused the Shuttle to fail to disengage from the air plane and when the thrusters ignited the 777 was still attached.

The 777 was dragged underneath the Shuttle as it hit close to the speed of sound causing the wings to be ripped off. Superman managed to disengage the shuttle pushing it safely into space this sending the plane plummeting towards the crowded Metropolis Park Stadium. Once the Shuttle was obviously safe Superman turned to save the 777 and reporters and crew on board it. Amazingly he managed to stop the plane just feet above the ground in the middle of the baseball field.

At the core of this amazing rescue is the relief the city of Metropolis feels with the return of Superman as

Superman has finally returned to Metropolis, hopefully to stay, and not a moment too soon.

pearance after 6 years Superman revealed he had travelled to his home planet of Krypton

and its population and was the reason why Superman was sent to Earth by his parents, who predicted the event would

whence he came, but as the shuttle and the plane rocketed into the earth's mesosphere, the passengers inside the jet reported seeing Superman fly past the left windows, and

the back of the plane, sending the Boeing jet into a supersonic downward spiral towards earth. The 777 with its passengers and crew were never in danger as Superman managed to stop the fuselage

Spectators in the stadium stands first recalled the rumbling noise of the 777 in its high speed descent towards them, before they saw the plummeting body of metal and human cargo. As the plane neared 20,000 feet it came into full view of the 120,000 spectators and near panic spread through the stadium in the attempt to run from the unknown point of impact.

When a small blur of color revealed the unlikely event of Superman's presence, the cries rolled around the stadium "Look it's Superman!", stopping the remaining crowd in their tracks. Thousands stood with mouths agape watching the rescue operation unfold before their disbelieving eyes. Thousands more returned to their seats as there was an obvious lack of impact of the plane with the ground.

As Superman gently swung the plane to safety in the middle of the diamond playing field, the onlooking crowd roared their approval and gratitude to Superman who, not heeding the praise, quickly released the pressure locked cabin doors to escort the passengers to the ground.

A few cuts and bruises were suffered by the press and officials, with most remaining unscathed. The plane itself did not escape unscathed with both of its wings torn off during its perilous plunge to earth. Given the speed with which the plane was falling to lose both wings under such intense pressure, it seems Superman's holiday from earth has not cost him any of his supernatural powers. Passengers on board the craft remember seeing the familiar red and blue hero fly past the window of the press cabin in a blur, as he flew to catch the nose of the plane and guide it to safety in the centre of the football stadium.

Too many of the passengers on board were in shock after being escorted from the battered Boeing's fuselage after it made contact with land to provide further details at this point in time.

Both US Air Force and Vir-

gin Galactic have not released an official statement about the cause of the malfunction in the launch sequence, but some experts have suggested the involvement of an EMP - Electro Magnetic Pulse device - as the incident coincided with a massive blackout that saw a loss of power to the entire eastern seaboard.

Metropolis welcomes Superman back with open arms!

An EMP unit releases an electromagnetic wave or pulse, much like a shock wave from a bomb blast, which disables any electronic device within its shock radius, including the most sophisticated and complex electronic systems used by government defense bodies.

If today's mysterious power failure was indeed a terrorist attack, no group as yet has claimed responsibility for the incident. At a press conference today, a US Air Force spokesperson stated that an investigation is underway, as residents of the wealthy metropolis suburb of Queens Park noticed a significant military presence in their neighborhood this afternoon. US Air Force representatives advised all Metropolis residents not to panic, as the military are conducting investigations in response to today's incident.

HPMs generate an intense "blast" of electromagnetic waves in the microwave frequency band (hundreds of megahertz to tens of gigahertz) that is strong enough to overload electrical circuits. Many types of matter are transparent to microwaves, including metallic objects, like those used in metal-oxide semiconductors, metal-semiconductors and polar devices, strong enough them, which in turn damages material.

Most likely, the United States' HPM e-bombs are really bombs at all, but probably more like some powerful microwave device that can generate a concentrated

(Continued on

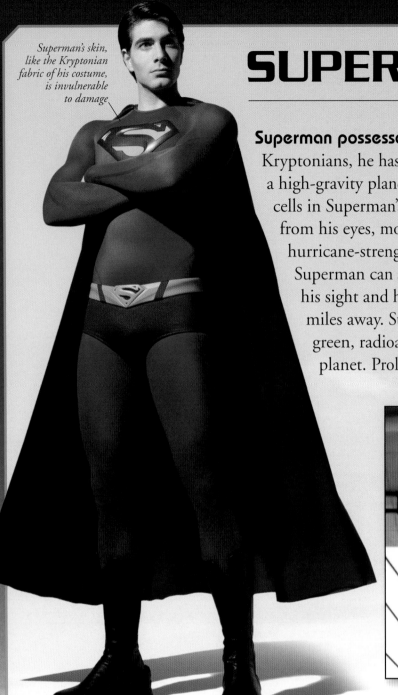

Superman's skin, like the Kryptonian fabric of his costume, is invulnerable to damage

SUPERMAN'S POWERS

Superman possesses abilities far beyond those of mortal men. Like all Kryptonians, he has a body that is incredibly strong, the result of evolving on a high-gravity planet. On Earth, the yellow rays of our sun super-charge the cells in Superman's body, allowing him to defy gravity, fire beams of heat from his eyes, move faster than the human eye can follow, and exhale a hurricane-strength gale or a super-cooled stream that freezes objects. Superman can see through almost anything with his X-ray vision, and his sight and hearing are so sharp that he can detect objects from many miles away. Superman loses his powers when exposed to kryptonite, a green, radioactive substance formed from the ruins of his native planet. Prolonged exposure will weaken him to the point of death.

Sentinel of Metropolis
Superman knew he could not waste his gifts, and refused to use them to dominate others. Instead, he uses his powers in the service of humankind, and hopes his example will inspire others to become heroes themselves.

EVERYDAY HERO
Superman's powers are perfect for halting natural disasters and other worldwide calamities, but wherever he can, the super hero also prevents smaller threats such as bank heists and purse snatchings. With his bulletproof skin, Superman is seldom in danger, but is challenged by the need to keep innocent bystanders from harm. Here, Superman confronts a robber holding up a diner in Metropolis. Stopping the villain is easy, but his first job is making sure no one gets hurt.

The owner waits for an opportunity to lunge for the gun

Smug and cocky, the crook prepares to fire

Superman poses for a photo with the diner owner. Following this incident, the grateful owner names a sandwich after the Man of Steel. Superman also has several streets and buildings named after him.

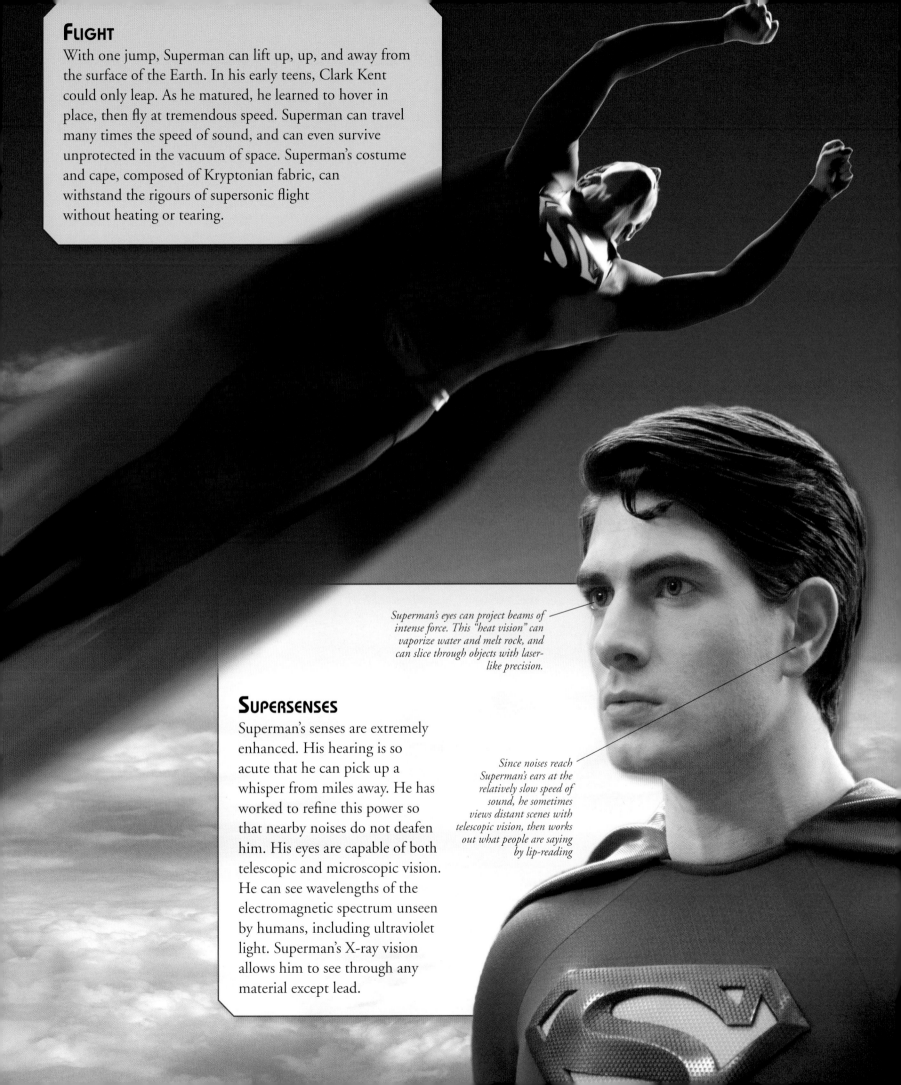

FLIGHT

With one jump, Superman can lift up, up, and away from the surface of the Earth. In his early teens, Clark Kent could only leap. As he matured, he learned to hover in place, then fly at tremendous speed. Superman can travel many times the speed of sound, and can even survive unprotected in the vacuum of space. Superman's costume and cape, composed of Kryptonian fabric, can withstand the rigours of supersonic flight without heating or tearing.

Superman's eyes can project beams of intense force. This "heat vision" can vaporize water and melt rock, and can slice through objects with laser-like precision.

SUPERSENSES

Superman's senses are extremely enhanced. His hearing is so acute that he can pick up a whisper from miles away. He has worked to refine this power so that nearby noises do not deafen him. His eyes are capable of both telescopic and microscopic vision. He can see wavelengths of the electromagnetic spectrum unseen by humans, including ultraviolet light. Superman's X-ray vision allows him to see through any material except lead.

Since noises reach Superman's ears at the relatively slow speed of sound, he sometimes views distant scenes with telescopic vision, then works out what people are saying by lip-reading

THE KENT FARM

⟨decorative glyphs⟩

Set amid the rural beauty of Smallville, Kansas, the Kent farm has been a family possession since 1871. Just one month before his graduation from Smallville High, Jonathan Kent inherited the farm from his own father. Sadly, the family line would end with Jonathan. His wife Martha could not conceive a child and so the couple adopted one that came to them from the stars. Jonathan always knew that a destiny greater than farming awaited his beloved son, Clark. Unfortunately, he never lived to see what Clark would go on to achieve, and died of a heart attack when the boy was just 17. This traumatic event propelled the young man to take the first steps into his new role as humanity's protector.

The windmill has withstood two tornadoes

THE HOMESTEAD

In the five years since Superman's sudden departure, the Kent farm has fallen on hard times. Never particularly profitable, the farm's cornfields have provided barely enough produce to pay for the farm's upkeep. Seasons of drought have left the soil parched and crumbled, and several farm buildings have fallen into disrepair. Even with the help of her partner Ben Hubbard, it's doubtful that Martha will be able to maintain the farm on her own.

Support structures house farming equipment

The Kent name is respected in Smallville, where it stands for honesty and hard work

The Kent farm is isolated, but always welcoming to visitors. Jonathan and Martha Kent's closest friends included the Hubbards and the Langs, whom they would invite over for dinner and conversation after the day's work in the fields was done. Smallville's social life is modest and quiet but the inhabitants like it that way.

Clark spent many nights stargazing on the porch, his imagination fired by the distant suns and the planets they harboured.

The family room of the main house is the scene of Clark's happiest memories. Reminders of his father – old photographs, the favourite chair, the books – are everywhere. In the kitchen, the table still bears Clark's name from the time he carved it into the wood as a young boy, much to Martha's annoyance at the time!

The branches of the drooping oak shelter a tree house, where Clark spent many boyhood afternoons

Sun and storms have left the main house in need of a fresh coat of paint

MARTHA KENT

Ben Hubbard provided emotional support to Martha following the death of her husband and the departure of her son, and the two struck up a romantic relationship. Martha and Ben spend many nights together, playing board games at home or bingo in town. With the guidance of Ben, who is an avid fisherman, Martha has even taken up fishing.

The Kansas horizon seems to stretch on for ever, making sunsets a spectacular vista of gold and red. Clark never sees views like this from the shadowed avenues of Metropolis.

Martha Kent is a championship Scrabble player

19

CRASH LANDING

∞⟡‼⬦⬧⬦⟡ ◊‼◊▢⊢•◊8

Superman's spaceship

screams back to Earth, arriving in the darkness of a Kansas night. Shattering the sound barrier and glowing with the heat of re-entry, the craft smashes into the cornfield behind the Kent farm. Much like the original Kryptonian baby pod, the craft lacks landing gear and comes to a stop only after ploughing out a deep furrow of soil. Superman, awakened from suspended animation by the ship's computer, disembarks at once to greet his mother. Weakened by his long journey and his near-fatal exposure to kryptonite, Superman collapses in Martha Kent's arms. She is overwhelmed to see her son again.

Unlike the bristles on the baby pod, the spaceship's spines are too thick to fold in on themselves during landing

Though Martha knows Clark has skin that can withstand bullets, she has no way of knowing what ordeals he may have suffered on his five-year journey. Her fear, upon seeing the devastation of the crash site, is that her son has been killed.

The stump of an oak tree once stood where the ship now rests, but it has been utterly obliterated by the impact. The intense heat radiating from the vessel's hull has set the fringes of the cornfield ablaze.

INFERNO

Martha Kent is playing Scrabble with Ben Hubbard when the booming trajectory of Superman's ship rattles the game board. Convincing a wary Ben that the disturbance is only a meteor, Martha jumps into her pickup truck and speeds to the scene of the crash. Rising smoke, tinged red by the glow of flames, reminds Martha of that long-ago crash that brought her a son.

Disorientated by the heat and darkness, Martha searches frantically for any sign of life. When Clark puts his hand on her shoulder, she nearly jumps out of her skin.

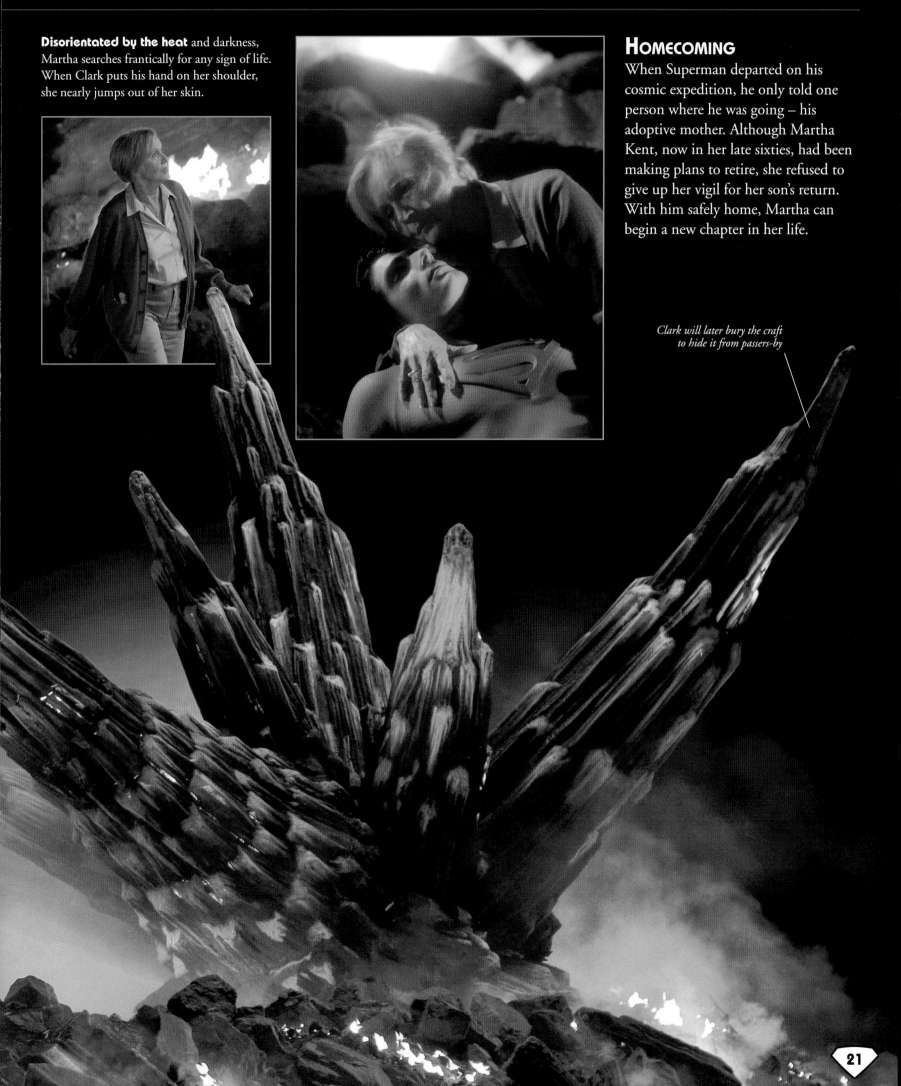

HOMECOMING

When Superman departed on his cosmic expedition, he only told one person where he was going – his adoptive mother. Although Martha Kent, now in her late sixties, had been making plans to retire, she refused to give up her vigil for her son's return. With him safely home, Martha can begin a new chapter in her life.

Clark will later bury the craft to hide it from passers-by

THE PLANET'S EXCHANGE RATES

Daily Planet

Metropolis' Greatest Newspaper

MONDAY, APRIL 5TH 1982   25 CENTS

VOL. LXII, NO. 24

VANDERWORTH TOPS THE FORTUNE 500!!

New Offer Was Never Made Public

MR VANDERWORTH IS PART OF ELITE WEALTHY

Vanderworth Tradition Of Corporate Success Lives On

Council Approves the Unbalanced Years Budget to Toughen US Spending Plans

More Breaking Stories Inside.

Steven Vanderworth, already rich from a shipping fortune made by his great-grandparents, used his business skill to expand the Vanderworth company into a vast international conglomerate. His wealth brought even more fame to Metropolis, and the city – including its newspaper, the *Daily Planet* – happily sang his praises.

LAST WILL

Gertrude Vanderworth, lonely ever since her husband Steven was taken before his time, has reached the end of her life. Because she was not born into wealth, Gertrude considers herself a self-made woman, which deepens her disgust for the relatives ("vultures", she calls them) who wait outside her bedroom door. In Lex Luthor, she sees a brilliant man worthy of a second chance, and will happily spite her family by giving him the entire Vanderworth fortune.

INHERITANCE

The moment his cell door slammed shut, Lex Luthor began plotting his return. It wasn't enough for him simply to win his freedom – Lex also wanted money to finance his plans for world domination. From prison he lost no time in writing love letters to Gertrude Vanderworth, controller of the immense Vanderworth fortune. The elderly widow soon fell for his charm and used her influence to secure his release. After marrying her, Lex presided over her final days. While her relatives waited outside the door, Lex made sure the dying woman gave him everything she owned.

Gertrude is breathing her last; only advanced medical equipment has got her this far

Lex needs only Gertrude's signature to become the richest man in Metropolis

WORLDLY TREASURES

In the years since her husband's death, Gertrude Vanderworth has spent millions of dollars building up her collection of paintings and sculptures. Possessed of immense wealth, but lacking any ability to recognize artistic talent, her purchases might uncharitably be called tacky. A series of oil paintings, done in a faux-18th century British style, depict Gertrude's beloved dogs, Tala and L.D., wearing diamond-studded collars. Until Lex Luthor arrived to woo her, Gertrude loved her dogs far more than any human. Ironically, it is her trusted Lex who will mistreat the pampered pets. If not for Lex's intervention, Gertrude would have left the entire Vanderworth fortune to the dogs.

Gertrude paid a fortune to have her pets painted in the style of English artist Constable

HOUSE WITHOUT TASTE

Located at 6 Springwood Drive in a wealthy area on the outskirts of Metropolis, the Vanderworth mansion is a generations-old family possession with a spectacular view of the waterfront. Gertrude Vanderworth has imposed her taste in art on the grounds, which are crowded with mismatched Greco-Roman statuary and intricate rococo knick-knacks. The interior of the house fares no better, displaying Gertrude's terrible paintings and expensive, tasteless furnishings.

This scam has required Lex to behave uncharacteristically kindly, a sensation he does not enjoy

LEX LUTHOR

His intellect is the only superpower he needs. Lex Luthor is the world's smartest man, and could have worked miracles for the people of Earth had he not desired to rule over them instead. With an IQ of 200, Lex amassed a fortune by the age of 25. In his most ambitious bid for domination, he tried to create a new coastline by sinking California, only to see his plans thwarted by Superman. Lex spent five years behind bars thanks to the Man of Steel. Now Lex is back, and hungry for revenge.

Daily Planet

SATURDAY, JULY 26TH 1997

LUTHOR GETS LIFE
THE LAW HAS FINALLY CAUGHT UP WITH THE INFAMOUS LEX LUTHOR – PUT AWAY FOR EVER!

DEBATES DELAYED YET AGAIN

Wanted for a host of crimes including robbery, murder, and terrorism, Lex Luthor was finally put away for good just over five years ago. But an army of lawyers laboured on Lex's appeal, and when Superman failed to testify against him, the way was clear for Lex's release.

Lex is a convincing defendant in the courtroom. Oratory was one of his earliest gifts and he has a good feel for how to manipulate people's emotions and baser instincts to his own advantage. But even this formidable skill wasn't enough to save him from a lengthy prison sentence after his first failed bid for world domination.

RISING STAR

Lex earned degrees from the best universities, and considered entering politics until he realized he could gain more power by bilking tycoons out of their hard-won fortunes. Lex's grandfather, who enriched LuthorCorp after World War II by seizing the assets of the debt-ridden American middle class, taught Lex to value land, calling it "the one thing they aren't making any more of". Lex took this advice to heart by executing a land grab that would have doomed California to a watery grave. Now he has a new plan, one that dwarfs all his previous atrocities put together.

Lex's piercing stare lets others know that they are in the presence of brilliance

Lex wears shades to avoid being recognized on the streets of Metropolis

MAN OF MEANS

To Lex, acquiring the Vanderworth fortune isn't about money. It's about freedom – the freedom to travel anywhere in the world with the Vanderworth yacht and helicopter, and the freedom to obtain even the rarest equipment to help him unlock the secrets of alien artifacts, such as the Fortress of Solitude. If his mad plans come to fruition, Lex will hold such power and wealth that traditional measurements for assets and influence will no longer have any meaning.

Lex believes that his appearance should reflect his status, and owns a wardrobe of custom-tailored clothing

Lex scarcely knew defeat until Superman appeared on Earth. The Man of Steel foiled Lex's every scheme, and Lex's thoughts have been consumed with a single, overriding obsession ever since: to kill Superman.

Lex is a self-taught expert in a dozen different sciences. After he met Superman, he learned everything there was to know about crystals and minerals, in the belief that Kryptonian technology held the key to his future supremacy.

VANITY

Lex considers himself superior to everyone around him, yet is vain enough to want others to act as a chorus that sings his praises. This has led Lex to surround himself with needy girlfriends and dull-witted henchmen, whose shortcomings make him more confident of his own dominance. Lex is a fan of mythology and opera, and views himself as a heroic figure willing to challenge the gods. A true megalomaniac, Lex has dreamed of world domination since he was a child. Ultimately, his vanity and his unwillingness to be contradicted by anyone are his greatest weaknesses.

Lex's "comb-over" wig has fallen out of favour

Lex's most obvious nod to vanity is the array of hair pieces he uses to hide his baldness. Not satisfied with either his natural appearance or with these artificial enhancements, Lex wears his insecurities on the top of his head.

KITTY KOWALSKI

Drawn into a relationship with the world's top criminal, Kitty Kowalski remains uncertain in her role as an accessory to evil. She first met Lex in prison while visiting her boyfriend, a small-time crook. Later, she witnessed Lex murder a fellow inmate. Kitty refused to squeal to the guards, and she and Lex made clear their attraction for each other. Kitty is an accomplished con artist, but begins to doubt her choices when confronted with Superman's honesty.

Kitty is happiest when
Lex recognizes and uses her talents, as when he ordered her to preoccupy Superman during the museum heist. But she is angered and hurt by Lex's constant disregard for her well-being.

Kitty rescues Mrs Vanderworth's dog from Lex's abuse

IN THE FAMILY
Kitty's mother married a string of rich businessmen, and fleeced all seven of them out of their money. Her daughter has tried to follow in mother's footsteps, but has never quite been able to remove her emotions from the equation.

Her role in the Lex Luthor caper shakes Kitty's determination. She has a lot to think about, and plenty of time in which to search her conscience.

PERSONALITY CLASH

She prefers Katherine, but Lex refuses to call her anything but Kitty – just one skirmish in the ongoing war of wills between the two lovers. Though contemptuous of Kitty for her "lesser intellect", Lex feels compelled to surround himself with hangers-on so he can flaunt his brilliance.

MULTIPLE IDENTITIES

Kitty, who has run many scams in the past, is skilled at donning a new set of clothes and acting the part of a different persona. While employed by Gertrude Vanderworth, she posed both as a maid and as a nurse. Later, she distracted the Man of Steel when she feigned sickness after he had stopped her out-of-control automobile. Kitty is also a devoted fan of movie costumes, particularly from the films of the 1940s and 1950s. She mixes and matches pieces from different eras to create her own signature style.

Wearing a wild ensemble
of zebra stripes, Kitty mixes Lex another vodka martini – with plenty of olives.

Kitty performed
no actual work in her role as a maid at the Vanderworth mansion, and the other members of the staff hated her. As soon as Lex took control of the mansion, she fired them all.

DOES THE WORLD NEED SUPERMAN?

The Daily Planet headline says it all: *Why the World Doesn't Need Superman.* In stark black and white, the article expresses every doubt that Superman has felt since he returned to Earth. The fact that it's written by Lois Lane only adds to his pain. Her story suggests that people who rely too much on a saviour become unable to save themselves. Superman, who has always tried to lead by inspiring others to greatness, realizes that his methods have been misinterpreted – especially after he abandoned his adopted planet to go on a fruitless quest for Krypton. In such a seemingly unfriendly world, does Superman still have a role?

Roots

Everywhere on Earth is important to Superman, but he feels a special connection with his hometown, Smallville. It was here that his superpowers first became apparent, including heat vision and the ability to fly. At Smallville High, Clark Kent made lifelong friendships with Pete Ross and Lana Lang. Memories are everywhere, but comfort is scarce. Returning to Smallville after five years is a bittersweet reminder of happier times.

A view of a beautiful sunset from the Kent farm isn't enough to ease the turmoil in Clark's heart. Lost in thought, he scans the glowing horizon and asks himself: What if Lois's article is right? Does my career as Superman end here? Do I even belong here now?

IN THE CELLAR

After adopting Clark, Jonathan and Martha Kent hid all the evidence of their son's otherworldly origins. The baby pod that brought Clark to Earth was packed away in a little-used cellar, hidden from Clark until his early teens. After the death of Jonathan Kent, the pod's father crystal – personally programmed by Jor-El – led Clark to the Arctic where it created the Fortress of Solitude.

Yellowed and frayed, a backlog of newspapers is just waiting to be read

Martha Kent began reading the *Daily Planet* when Clark got his first job as a reporter. She still bought the newspaper while Clark was away, and now has five years of copies stacked in the barn.

Past issues of the *Daily Planet*, including some from Superman's early heroic career, provide Clark with a sample of changing public attitudes towards Metropolis's guardian. *Caped Wonder Stuns City* was the first story, followed by Lois Lane's account of their rooftop meeting, *I Spent the Night With Superman*. Although most stories are positive, it is Lois's *Why the World Doesn't Need Superman* that affects Clark most deeply.

Out of touch for five years, Clark gets up to speed on current affairs

ARCTIC QUEST

Lex doesn't waste any time. Immediately after seizing the Vanderworth fortune, he embarks on a polar expedition to seek out Superman's Fortress of Solitude. The yacht *Gertrude* is his command centre, equipped with advanced navigation technology and crewed by four thugs Lex recruited from prison. Although the *Gertrude* wasn't built for Arctic conditions, it is still a powerful vessel, and nimbly makes its way through the icy waters en route to a remote glacial shelf. As the view from the bridge grows increasingly bleak and inhospitable, Lex's henchmen begin to wonder if their boss has lost his mind.

The yacht's elegant stateroom provides a welcome contrast to the freezing fury outside. Through the glass-panelled floor, a view of dark waters stretches into the depths. Occasionally a pale fish swims into view, the only sign of life in this desolate part of the world.

THROUGH THE STORM

Lex, who has been to the Fortress of Solitude before, has embarked on this search with little more than his memories to guide him. More precise information has proven elusive. Even high-resolution satellite photos of the Arctic show nothing – only localized storms of blowing snow. Lex suspects that the unusual weather patterns may themselves be evidence of Kryptonian technology.

Guided by GPS instruments, the yacht searches for signs of civilization

LEX'S HENCHMEN

Behind bars, Lex met all sorts of unsavoury people. By attracting followers, he rose to the top of the prison hierarchy, and murdered anyone who stood in his way. Brutus, Riley, Stanford, and Grant each have talents that Lex finds useful, and each came up for parole – or arranged a jailbreak – at the same time Lex was released. In addition to their practical talents, the henchmen provide Lex Luthor with the satisfaction of knowing that he is the smartest person in the room.

Brutus is a rock, able to withstand any blow without flinching and knock out any opponent with a single punch. An ex-mercenary, Brutus is skilled with firearms and heavy explosives. For Lex, this guy's muscles are the main thing that matter – which is just as well, because Brutus wouldn't win any prizes for brains.

JOURNEY INTO THE UNKNOWN

The yacht is designed for operation by a larger crew, and its emptiness only makes the Arctic outside seem more desolate. Kitty doubts privately that they'll find anything. Brutus and Riley are itching to start hurting people. Stanford is confident that they're on the right course, but worries that rough seas may damage the vessel. Lex has no doubt of success. He considers the yacht expendable, as long as it gets him to his destination.

Grant, hired for his ability to follow orders, acts as the ship's lookout

Riley takes a break from filming and hopes that the boss doesn't notice

With growing confidence, Lex scans the darkness for a sign of the familiar

Stanford takes the wheel, certain of Lex's ability to deliver what he has promised

Kitty is having second thoughts, but knows it's too late to back out now

Riley is a sadistic killer with a love of cinema. Prior to prison, he used to film live executions for paying customers. Riley was eager to join the mission so that he could have a ringside seat at Lex's killings. Lex orders him to film every moment of the voyage, believing that the footage will be important to history.

Stanford was a rare find among the prison inmates – a self-taught mineralogist and astronomer with a genius-level IQ and a special talent for understanding the significance of crystal power. Stanford is the only one of the henchmen with full knowledge of Lex's evil scheme.

THE YACHT GERTRUDE

Lex's biggest prize from scamming his way into the billion-dollar Vanderworth fortune is the *Gertrude*, a luxury yacht designed to be a floating mansion. Commissioned by Steven Vanderworth and named in honour of his beloved wife, the *Gertrude* has state-of-the-art electronic systems and every type of indulgence, such as in-cabin jacuzzis and a fully stocked bar in the main stateroom. Its engines are powerful enough to push the craft through chunky sheets of ice. Lex uses the *Gertrude* as a mobile headquarters, travelling from the Arctic to the mid-Atlantic in a style befitting his status as the planet's would-be ruler.

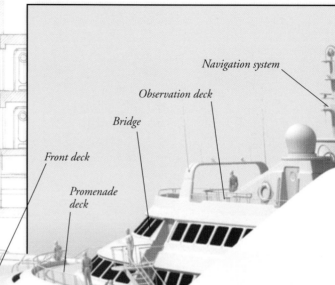

Navigation system

Observation deck

Bridge

Front deck

Promenade deck

LAP OF LUXURY

This desk, originally used by Steven Vanderworth to manage his shipping empire, looks across the enormous stateroom located on the yacht's lowest deck. In this inviting space, visitors can page though the books in the library, play the antique grand piano, or listen to operatic arias through the yacht's sound system. The glass bottom offers a spectacular view of the undersea depths, and light refracting from below fills the room with a pleasing glow. For the most part, the yacht's decor is tasteful, an attribute not found in the home of Gertrude Vanderworth.

Gertrude Vanderworth didn't spend much time on the yacht after her husband's death, so signs of her taste in decor are absent. The master suite is an exception, containing telltale portraits of Gertrude's beloved dogs.

As soon as Lex Luthor commandeered the yacht's master suite, he filled it with personal items, including his collection of hairpieces. Lex has a variety of styles to suit his moods, ranging from relaxed to murderous.

The hallways of the *Gertrude* are lined with polished teak floorboards. On a ship this size, it is easy to get lost on the way from the bridge to the engine room.

TONNAGE: 1,400	
SPEED: 65 Kn	
LENGTH: 91 m (300 Ft)	
BEAM: 17 m (58 Ft)	
HORSE POWER: 12,000	

The yacht, custom-built for Steven Vanderworth by a Greek shipwright, has 16 cabins that can accommodate more than 32 guests. It is propelled by twin Caterpillar diesel engines. The sheer size and opulence of the *Gertrude* sparked a competitive yacht-buying frenzy among the billionaires in Mr. Vanderworth's social circle.

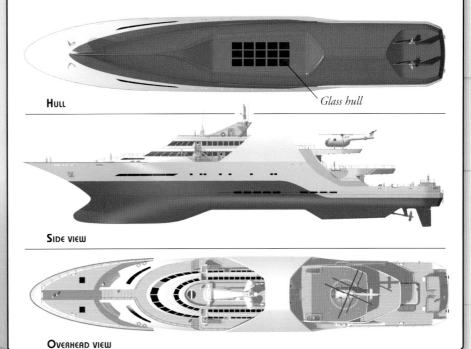

HULL

Glass hull

SIDE VIEW

OVERHEAD VIEW

Helicopter

Helicopter landing pad

Mid-level deck

Pool

Stern deck

Stern

Steven and Gertrude took very few trips aboard their yacht. Only on rare occasions did they take friends on tours of the Mediterranean or on cruises along the US eastern seaboard. After her husband's death, Gertrude left the yacht moored in Metropolis harbour, fully staffed but unused.

Drive screw

Rudder

THE FORTRESS OF SOLITUDE

The crystalline lattice of the Fortress rises from the surrounding ice like the spires of an alien cathedral. Not even polar bears prowl this part of the Arctic, making it a lonely outpost indeed.

At the age of 17, Clark Kent left Smallville and journeyed north. Guided by Jor-El's father crystal, Clark reached a desolate spot near the Arctic Circle's Fletcher Abyssal Plain. Using the crystal as a seed, he watched a vast Kryptonian structure assemble itself in minutes. Inside this Fortress of Solitude, the holographic ghosts of Jor-El and Lara told their son of Krypton's vanished glories, and warned him to use his powers to inspire the people of Earth, not to rule over them. The Fortress contains wonders of Kryptonian technology, including a device for projecting individuals into the extra-dimensional Phantom Zone, and doubles as a repository for souvenirs Superman has collected from across the solar system.

VOICES FROM THE GRAVE

Although Clark learned the values of truth and justice from the Kents, it was his instruction in the Fortress of Solitude under the ghostly guidance of Jor-El and Lara that convinced him to take up the mantle of Superman. Returning to the Fortress whenever he needs to see his birth parents, Superman finds it comforting to hear their words, but he knows that he is only listening to recordings selected by computer.

DESECRATION

Only a few people – Lois Lane and Lex Luthor among them – had ever set foot in the Fortress of Solitude prior to Superman's departure from Earth. After his return, Superman journeys to the Fortress and discovers a terrible crime. Approximately ten crystals, including the all-important father crystal programmed by Jor-El himself, have vanished, and with them the secrets to Kryptonian crystal building. Superman knows of only one man with the resources and brainpower to pull off such a brazen theft.

Control panels are operated by raising or lowering crystals, or by inserting new crystals into the control-board

Standard Kryptonian memory crystal

Kryptonian crystals of the type stolen by Lex Luthor are designed to store vast amounts of data, including holographic recordings and interactive star charts. In addition, they carry instructions for self-replication through the transformation of raw material. A single crystal gave rise to the Fortress of Solitude, and Lex has an even greater construction project in mind.

HUNT FOR THE CRYSTAL

Lex Luthor and Superman go back a long way. Over the years Lex has learned quite a few of the Man of Steel's secrets. With Superman away on a journey to Krypton, Lex has been eager to exploit some of those secrets for his own evil ends – but his prison sentence and his courtship of the widow Vanderworth have delayed his plans. Now at last, Lex has returned to Superman's Fortress of Solitude where he hopes to obtain an object of immense power. Accompanied by his henchmen and Kitty, he must first find the remote citadel, decipher its alien technology, and steal the tools that will give him the power to rule the Earth – that is, if he doesn't freeze to death first.

Kitty paged through several books on Hollywood adventure movies before selecting her polar ensemble. Now she's wishing she'd chosen something less glamorous and more practical.

Lex's thugs privately grumble that they didn't sign up for sub-zero orienteering

Lex, who has been inside the Fortress before, carefully retraces his steps

NO VISITORS

In addition to its remoteness in an unexplored part of the Arctic, the Fortress of Solitude is shielded from prying eyes by an artificial storm that swirls snow and ice around the stronghold's perimeter. These camouflaging winds act as Superman's security system and early-warning notice. This time, however, Superman is not staying in the Fortress, and is not warned of the intruders' entry.

The route to the Fortress of Solitude is nearly impassable. After anchoring the *Gertrude*, and realizing that the gale-force winds will prevent aerial exploration by helicopter, Lex and company proceed on foot. During the arduous trek, Lex's discovery of an offshoot crystal from the Fortress's foundation proves he's on the right path.

CRYSTAL SCIENCE

Lex has spent much of the previous five years studying crystals, and waiting for the day when he could use Superman's own technology against him. He has amassed a library of books on the subject, as well as innumerable magazine articles and laboratory papers. Stanford has also stolen some rare crystal specimens.

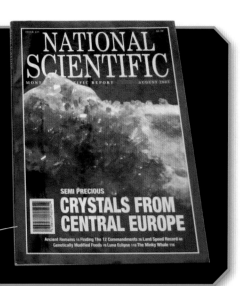

Periodicals such as this frequently report on both crystals and meteorites

Kryptonian memory crystal, loaded with the accumulated wisdom of Krypton's greatest scientists

To a person of Lex's genius, the alien control panels are easily understood

THE GRAND TOUR

Superman's Fortress of Solitude is an enormous structure. Lex and the others survey every corner, recording the journey with Riley's video camera. Lex lingers in a cavernous chamber he dubs "the garage", where he sees evidence of the construction and launch of Superman's spaceship. The nerve centre of the Fortress is its crystal control room. Here, Lex conjures up the holographic ghost of Superman's father Jor-El, who recites pre-programmed lectures on the secrets of crystal technology.

LOIS AND CLARK

Lois scans for a taxi, and, as usual, avoids looking Clark in the eyes

He has been a rival, a colleague, and a friend, but never a lover. Clark Kent's decision to adopt a sweetly awkward disguise at the Daily Planet helps deflect attention from his activities as Superman, but it puts a wall between him and the woman he loves. At first, the relationship between Clark Kent and Lois Lane was one of amused competition, as Lois adjusted to the new reporter from the farmlands of Kansas. She soon grew to respect Clark as a writer, then treasured him as a confidante who always lent a sympathetic ear.

LOIS AND SUPERMAN

In years past, Lois loved Superman – a sharp contrast to the brotherly friendship she shares with Clark. A rooftop meeting, reminiscent of their first flight together, reminds Lois and Superman of the love they once shared. While Lois seems to be enamoured with Superman's heroism, she is actually responding to Clark's inner character. But an honest relationship will never occur while Clark keeps his true self hidden behind his bumbling persona.

Clark always pulls back when he is close to making an emotional connection

When the subject turns to Superman's absence from Earth, Lois pours out her feelings to Clark. She is hurt that Superman left without even saying goodbye, and she vents her frustrations in an angry rush aimed straight at Clark. Although Clark longs to tell Lois the truth, he knows that he can't.

SUPERMAN'S OUTFIT

It is one of the most recognized uniforms in the world – the red, yellow, and blue suit that announces the arrival of the Man of Steel. Made years ago by Martha Kent from Kryptonian materials found in Superman's baby pod, the costume is highly resistant to damage and is close-fitting to allow for unrestricted, superspeed movement. The outfit has changed slightly during Superman's career, but remains an iconic symbol of heroism, strength, and sacrifice.

The suit is hidden, but accessible

During his first week back in Metropolis, Clark carries his costume in his suitcase. He has not yet decided whether to return to his former life as a super hero, but events will soon help him make up his mind.

The fabric is uniquely Kryptonian – insulating, tough, and stretchy; it is unlike anything found on Earth

SECRET IDENTITY

To most, it is inconceivable that Superman – an alien with powers undreamed of by humans – would have an identity other than his public one. The fact that he makes no effort to conceal his face behind a mask only reinforces this belief. In truth, Superman always travels with his costume while posing as Clark Kent, and can change out of his street clothing at superspeed.

The insignia on Superman's chest, commonly thought to be a capital letter S, is actually the serpentine crest of Krypton's House of El. It symbolizes a pledge to renounce the dishonesty and violence that marred Krypton's past.

To the people of Earth, this Kryptonian crest has become synonymous with Superman

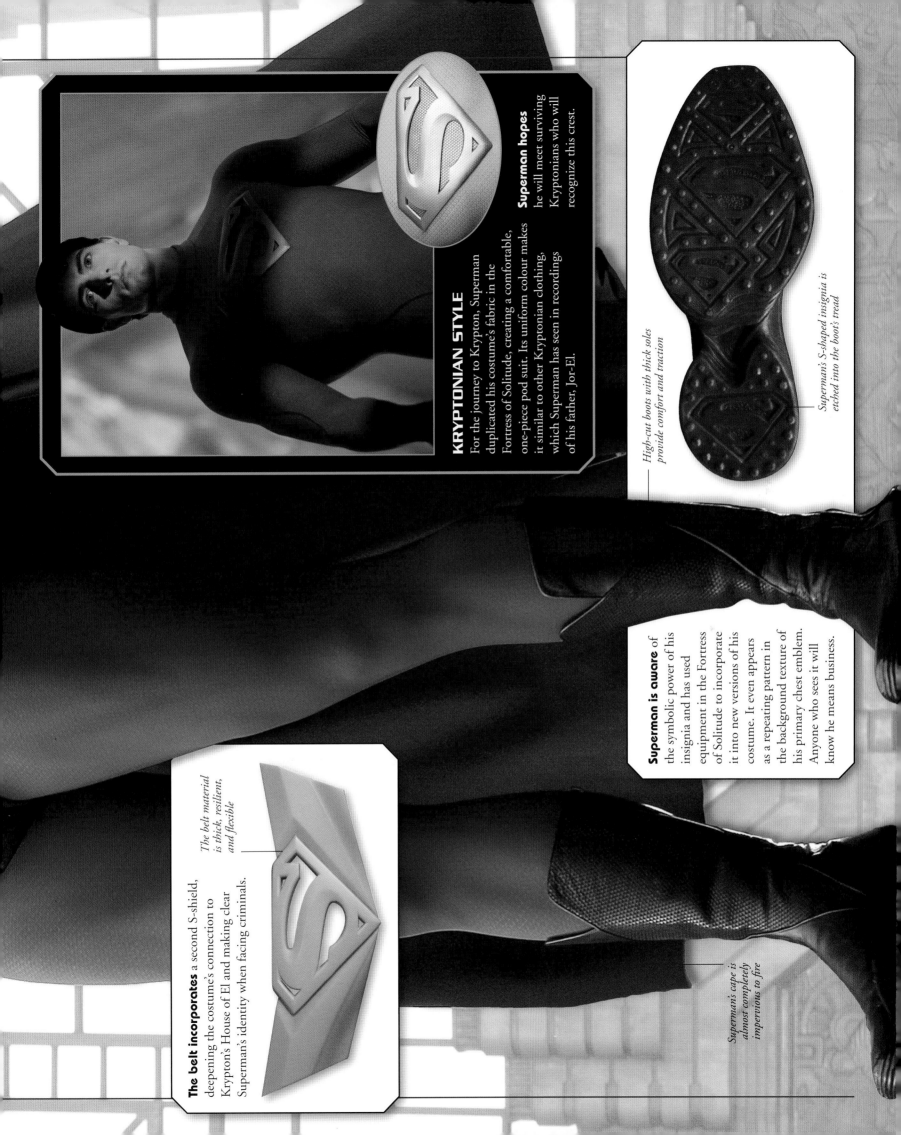

KRYPTONIAN STYLE

For the journey to Krypton, Superman duplicated his costume's fabric in the Fortress of Solitude, creating a comfortable, one-piece pod suit. Its uniform colour makes it similar to other Kryptonian clothing, which Superman has seen in recordings of his father, Jor-El.

Superman hopes he will meet surviving Kryptonians who will recognize this crest.

High-cut boots with thick soles provide comfort and traction

Superman's S-shaped insignia is etched into the boot's tread

Superman is aware of the symbolic power of his insignia and has used equipment in the Fortress of Solitude to incorporate it into new versions of his costume. It even appears as a repeating pattern in the background texture of his primary chest emblem. Anyone who sees it will know he means business.

The belt incorporates a second S-shield, deepening the costume's connection to Krypton's House of El and making clear Superman's identity when facing criminals.

The belt material is thick, resilient, and flexible

Superman's cape is almost completely impervious to fire

METROPOLIS: CITY OF TOMORROW

It is one of the world's great cities, home to strivers, dreamers, and one amazing super hero. Founded as a trading port on the North American eastern seaboard, Metropolis has become a hub of news, commerce, and culture for the United States and for the world. The heart of Metropolis is an urban island, home to the *Daily Planet* and famous neighbourhoods such as ritzy Bakerline and destitute Suicide Slum. Downtown Metropolis is known for its architecture, boasting a skyline of soaring buildings built over the past 200 years. A welcoming city for immigrants, Metropolis encourages innovation, and futuristic technology usually appears here first before spreading elsewhere. The overall atmosphere in the city is one of optimism, with an industrious population that looks to the future.

The Museum of Natural History has stood in the heart of the city for over 130 years

Tourists and school groups regularly visit Metropolis's cultural institutions

Shiny glass and steel office towers came with the city's modernist era

TIMELESS CITY

Metropolis has a timeless feel, due to its straightforward blending of styles both classic and modern. The city's most prominent buildings are products of the skyscraper boom of the 1920s and 1930s, and have the streamlined, art deco embellishments typical of that era.

Statue of Civil War general Amos Vanderworth

Pre-war constructions give the city's skyline much of its character

STOP

SCHOOL BU

STOP

The globe is used by Metropolitans to get their bearings while navigating the crowded city blocks

At 65 storeys, the Daily Planet building is one of the taller structures erected during its era

Hailing from an era before air-con, every window in the Daily Planet building opens to the outside

THE DAILY PLANET

It's not quite the tallest building in Metropolis, but it's easily the most famous. The globe at the top of the *Daily Planet* building has glittered for over 70 years, representing the beauty of the city and the ideals for which the newspaper was founded. The *Daily Planet* has existed in some form or another since the earliest days of Metropolis, but the erection of the skyscraper prior to the outbreak of World War II was the event that established the Planet as the foremost newspaper of the nation. Currently helmed by editor-in-chief Perry White, the *Daily Planet* stands strong as one of the world's most respected institutions.

The newspaper's logo has undergone subtle changes over the decades to keep it current

TITAN OF INDUSTRY

The *Daily Planet* building has a wide base for stability and deep grooves in its sides to let more light into the interior. Jack Mayer, the *Daily Planet's* publisher at the time of the building's dedication, flipped the switch that illuminated the globe at the culmination of a day of festivities and parades in 1932. Although the *Daily Planet* newspaper is the building's largest tenant, hundreds of smaller businesses rent office space on the lower floors.

The Daily Planet competes with several rivals in the newsstands of Metropolis, but always has the edge through its use of dramatic photos and screaming headlines. The Planet seldom uses one exclamation point when two will work better!

A miniature replica of the *Daily Planet* globe adorns the plaza outside the main entrance. Hundreds of workers pass through the revolving doors each day. Thousands more circulate through the subway station in Shuster Square opposite the plaza.

Art deco, popular in the decade when the *Daily Planet* building was designed, is a jazzy style expressed with stepping patterns and streamlined contours. The lobby is packed with art deco ornamentation, from the ornate clock to the zig-zagging wall overlays.

These structures, called dendriform columns, provide perches for flat-screen televisions

Set into the lobby floor, this seal marking the building's dedication reads *Daily Planet, Established 1932.*

Staffers leave work piled high over their desks

WHERE THE ACTION IS

In contrast to the hectic energy of the reporters who work there, the bullpen is an elegant area that uses architectural tricks to create the illusion of open space. The room's columns have wide flares set beneath the ceiling, making it appear that nothing but air supports the room. The Planet's reporters work at desks packed tightly across the floor, and glass-fronted offices line the walls on both sides. Perry White's office sits at the end, directly opposite the elevator bank, and looks out on the city below.

18 Pages Today

Daily Planet EXTRA!

HINDENBURG IN FLAMES!!

THE HINDENBURG WAS A SKELETON IN ONLY 37 SECONDS

36 DEAD
120 INJURED

LEADING THE WAY

The *Daily Planet* has reported on every major story of the past century. Its most memorable front pages are on display throughout the building. From the sinking of the Titanic to Neil Armstrong's walk on the moon, the Planet's corridors double as halls of history.

WELCOME TO THE BULLPEN

The Daily Planet bullpen is a hive of activity, buzzing with the hubbub of Metropolis's best journalists all trying to get their stories filed in time for the morning edition. The fearsome Perry White is their dictatorial editor-in-chief. As the staffers step from the elevators into the bullpen, framed front pages remind them of the *Daily Planet's* greatest headlines. Reporters tap away on their keyboards as overhead screens broadcast breaking news 24 hours a day. With the return of the Man of Steel, the bullpen has become busier than ever.

Perry holds court in one of his daily staff meetings

Staff meetings at the *Daily Planet* are one-sided affairs – Perry assigns new stories, then demands updates on the stories he handed out the day before. Some staffers dread the meetings. Others consider them the quickest way to win their boss's good opinion.

Ironically, given how many times he barks, "Don't call me Chief", Perry's mug bears the image of an Indian chief

STAR REPORTER

Perry was happy to add Lois Lane to his staff, thinking that her family's military background would provide useful journalist contacts. Lois quickly became one of his top reporters. Perry always expected great things from Lois, and when her reporting won her the Pulitzer Prize his confidence in her was vindicated. Now he couldn't manage without her.

Competition among Daily Planet reporters is fierce. Unlike their more sober rivals at the *Metropolis Times*, the Planet reporters have been ordered to deliver startling, headline-worthy copy every day. Nothing is more important to Perry White than selling newspapers, and no story sells bigger than Superman.

Lois, annoyed that the meeting is taking time away from her writing, is only half-listening

PERRY WHITE

Perry White, the *Daily Planet's* editor-in-chief, has been a newspaperman since he began making bicycle deliveries as a boy. In his teens, he lied about his age to get a reporting job at a Cleveland newspaper, and three years later he found work in London as a foreign correspondent. After writing a bestselling book about his overseas adventures, Perry married and fathered his first child. Family responsibilities prompted him to settle down in Metropolis, and he began his career at the *Daily Planet* as an assistant editor. During his time at the Planet, Perry has used punchy headlines and splashy photos to boost newsstand sales, but he never stoops to the level of cheap tabloid gossip. He remains a hero to many journalists in Metropolis.

Now in his mid-60s, Perry can look back on a satisfying career spent bringing the truth and good journalism to the masses.

Perry makes no apologies for his tough attitude. He hires the best and expects the best in return. Under his decades-long tenure as editor-in-chief, the *Daily Planet's* circulation has doubled. Despite frequent rows with the Planet's shareholders, they respect his judgment.

The office's fixtures are in the same art deco style as the building itself

Perry's office is adjacent to the bullpen floor, and looks out over the Metropolis skyline through a panoramic window. Flanking the vista are two decorative rams' heads that adorn the building's exterior. Perry's bookcase holds leather-bound back issues of the *Daily Planet*, and framed journalism awards hang on the wall.

LOIS LANE

𝖔𝖎⫫–·⊗ 𝖔𝖎‼◇ӟ

Lois Lane, the Daily Planet's star reporter, is renowned for her stubbornness as an investigator. Her quirks include atrocious spelling and an inability to quit her dependence on cigarettes. Lois always landed the biggest Superman stories, and once enjoyed a romantic relationship with the Man of Steel. But after Superman's abrupt departure, Lois found new love with Richard White.

Daily Planet
METROPOLIS' GREATEST NEWSPAPER

LOIS LANE
SENIOR REPORTER
ID NO - 052667582

PRESS

Lois met Superman when he saved her from a helicopter crash. After their rooftop meeting, she published Superman's first interview. The two became involved, which only deepened Lois's hurt when Superman left without saying goodbye. Lois has moved on with her life, but after Superman's return, the two realize how much they still care for each other.

Despite not seeing Clark in five years, Lois quickly slips back into her old habit of treating him as a likeable background figure. Lois complains to him that she has been asked to write another story about Superman.

The couple's home is a gallery to their competing collections of artwork

WATERFRONT LIVING

After the birth of her son, Lois moved from downtown Metropolis to the western suburbs. She and Richard share a spacious home on the shores of the Metropolis River. Richard ties his seaplane to the dock out back. The couple commute separately to the *Daily Planet* offices, but somehow find the time to pick Jason up from school.

RICHARD WHITE

Perry White's nephew Richard is an assistant editor at the *Daily Planet*. Formerly based at the newspaper's offices in London, he returned to Metropolis to head its international bureau. Richard and Lois soon fell in love. When Richard decided to stay in Metropolis permanently, the two became engaged.

Richard is protective of Jason's fragile health

Richard knows that Lois and Superman once shared a romance, and that he should feel jealous over it. But in truth, he has always looked up to Superman, and admires what he did for Metropolis.

JIMMY OLSEN

•8—◇⟨⟩⬧⟨⟩⬧| ‖•◇⬧⬧⬧◇

Many people have changed in the five years that Superman has been absent from Earth, but Jimmy Olsen still has a smile for his old friend Clark Kent. A junior photographer for the *Daily Planet*, Jimmy's irrepressible personality and trademark bow ties make him a likeable figure in the newsroom. After years spent working as a table boy, copy boy, and assistant, he finally won Perry White's approval to shoot full-time for the Planet less than a year ago, but is now tormented by his failure to capture even a single image of Superman on film.

Thanks to his days delivering coffee from floor to floor, Jimmy knows almost everyone on the *Daily Planet* staff. He is Lois Lane's unofficial assistant, and a constant irritant to Perry White due to his habit of calling the editor as "Chief".

BEHIND THE LENS

Jimmy had his first photos published in the Metropolis publication *The Clearview Shopper* during his teens. This led to a post with his high-school yearbook, and from there, an internship at the *Daily Planet*. Jimmy imagined himself becoming the Planet's crime-beat photographer.

Jimmy puts his modest salary towards the purchase of top-notch camera equipment

Jimmy is the first to greet Clark upon his return to the *Daily Planet* bullpen. He even made a welcome-back cake. Over the past few years, Jimmy has received many postcards from "Clark", which were actually sent by Martha Kent to maintain the fiction about her son's international travels. One of the funniest cards concerned an imaginary Peruvian llama race.

CATALYST

Although he doesn't let his cheerful mask slip in the *Daily Planet* building, Jimmy is frustrated that he hasn't had the career break that he's been working so hard to achieve. While catching up with Clark inside the Ace O' Clubs, Jimmy witnesses the live TV coverage of the disaster that has overcome the *Explorer* space shuttle mission. The shock of the catastrophe makes Jimmy realize that the time for self-pity is past, and if he's going to break out of his slump, he's going to have to do it himself. If only he could take that photograph that would make his career.

The only thing Perry White wants is an exclusive photo of Superman, but Jimmy can't capture anything more than a blur. Even a boy with a cell phone scoops him, scoring a front-page shot of Superman rescuing of an out-of-control motorist. But Clark's friendship gives Jimmy new confidence, and he keeps his eyes open for his One Big Shot.

THE RETURN OF CLARK KENT: REPORTER

⬦⬦⬦ ⬦⬦⬦⬦⬦ ⬦⬦⬦ ⬦⬦⬦⬦⬦ ⬦⬦⬦⬦

Despite Clark's long absence, Perry White rehires him at his former level of Senior Reporter.

The Clark Kent who calls Smallville home has always been Superman's truest self – but in order to separate his super hero persona from his home life he has adopted a third identity. "Clark Kent, reporter" is the good-natured, bumbling guise that Clark wears in the *Daily Planet* newsroom, and it is the only identity familiar to Lois, Jimmy, and Perry. The disguise includes glasses, a higher-pitched voice, and a nervous stammer, but even with this exaggerated version of himself, Clark's good heart shines through. After five years away, Clark Kent, reporter, returns to the *Daily Planet*. Lois doesn't suspect his true identity, even though his return coincides with that of Superman.

The Daily Planet is the perfect place for Clark to hear about unfolding disasters, and determine which ones look like jobs for Superman.

CLARK REHIRED

Clark won a place on the *Daily Planet* staff due to his love of writing and his drive to seek out the truth (Perry White also called him "the fastest typist I've ever seen".) Perry was able to rehire Clark because of a vacancy left by the death of staffer Norm Palmer. Although Clark is accustomed to tackling challenges head-on, he isn't sure how to adjust to the passage of time. The *Daily Planet* has become a different place since he went away.

Clark leaves this suitcase (containing his Superman costume) in the janitor's closet

WELCOME BACK

Jimmy Olsen is the first to greet Clark upon his return to the newsroom, and the only one to show genuine excitement. Clark's fellow reporters, including Lois, are too busy to offer more than a quick "welcome back". Re-establishing his identity as a newspaper reporter is the first step on Clark's journey back to normality, but some of the changes that have occurred in his absence shock him.

A photo on Lois's desk tells Clark that his former love now has a young son. Lois's life hasn't stood still, and Clark, as Superman, can't simply pick things up from where they were when he left.

HIGH FLYER

When she first met Clark, Lois was sceptical of the Smallville native's homespun modesty. But Clark quickly proved himself a top investigative reporter, competing with Lois to bring in the biggest scoops on government corruption and the outrages of criminal mastermind Lex Luthor. Perry White considered Lois and Clark – with photographer Jimmy Olsen often tagging along – to be his best team. Martha Kent was proud to know that a Clark Kent byline was the mark of a good story, and many of Clark's colleagues considered him to be on a career path that would soon net him a Pulitzer. Perry never understood Clark's motives for leaving at the height of his success, but is glad to have one of his best reporters back in the fold.

With his superhuman eyes, Clark can see equally well with or without his glasses. But his colleagues don't know that.

THE ACE O' CLUBS

ᛏᛟᚷᛁ ᛁᛟᛟᚷᛁ ᛁᛁᚨ ᛟᛟᚷᛁᚲᛁᛟᚨᚨ ᛁᛟᛁᚷ

It's been a Metropolis fixture for nearly a century. Located a block from the *Daily Planet* building and close to the boxing gyms that dot this section of the city, the Ace O' Clubs is a comfortable watering hole for Metropolitans from all walks of life. During the 1930s and '40s, the Ace O' Clubs regularly played host to boxing royalty, including Joe Louis and Ted Grant, and today it still welcomes champs and contenders from the fight arena of the Metropolis Hotel Ballroom. Lately, Jimmy Olsen has been coming to the Ace O' Clubs on his lunch breaks, drowning his sorrows over what he considers to be his stagnating career.

BO "BIBBO" BIBBOWSKI

Bo has tended bar at the Ace O' Clubs for decades, and remembers every face that has ever sat opposite him on a barstool. A former longshoreman and boxer, Bo is the soul of the place, and decorates the bar with fight posters advertising upcoming bouts. He is a huge fan of the Man of Steel, considering Superman to be the toughest guy ever to walk the streets. Bo also has a soft spot for the down-on-their-luck, holding a special fondness for ex-boxers like himself. Recently, he has befriended his new regular Jimmy Olsen, seeing something strangely familiar about the junior photographer.

Clark's super-charged metabolism is not affected by alcohol

Jimmy is upset over not having had a photo published in nearly two months

The Ace O' Clubs isn't known for its food – Jimmy jokes that it serves up "a great plate of pretzels and peanuts"

On weekends, the bar fills with a volatile mix of local toughs and young club-goers

Bo always clears a barstool for the regulars at the Ace O' Clubs

Boxing memorabilia, some of it dating from the 19th century, decorates the bar's dark corners

Bo doesn't remember ever seeing Clark Kent in the Ace O' Clubs before

Despite its reputation as a dive bar, the Ace O' Clubs is clean and well-maintained

Jimmy, eager to catch up with Clark and commiserate over the unfortunate changes in their lives, suggests a long stopover at the Ace O' Clubs. When the bar's overhead TV reports on the unfolding *Explorer* shuttle disaster, Clark is immediately spurred into action – but not before picking up the tab. The dumbfounded Jimmy watches the screen as Clark makes his excuse to leave.

POWER SURGE

◇•⫴⫴•∞⫶⟅ ⬙ïⵗ8⫶

The miniature railroad set that fills the basement of the Vanderworth mansion provides a small-scale model backdrop for a demonstration of Kryptonian technology. The results of the experiment far surpass Lex Luthor's wildest dreams. Once the crystals' power is activated, it becomes clear that a chain reaction will send out an electromagnetic pulse across half the country, knocking out everything from car starters to cell phones. As a rolling blackout envelops the railroad set, Lex is treated to the apocalyptic sight of the crystals growing, multiplying, and finally obliterating the tiny model landscape.

Lex gazes into the transparent heart of one of his stolen crystals. What looks like a humble mineral is actually an alien technological artifact light years more advanced than anything found on Earth.

Stanford waits for Lex's signal

KNOWLEDGE IS POWER

Without the data taken from the Fortress of Solitude, the stolen crystals would be useless to Lex. But armed with the secret information, he can recreate the vanished glories of Kryptonian science. Stanford, a gifted mineralogist, is the only member of Lex's crew who understands the implications of the boss's plan.

Only a tiny sliver of crystal is needed for this trial. If it works, Lex has much grander plans in mind.

VANDERWORTH RAILROAD

Steven Vanderworth, incredibly rich from his shipping interests, had a hobbyist's obsession with model railroads. His fortune paid for one of the finest miniature railroads in the world, with loops of track snaking through detailed recreations of famous landmarks, including the Swiss Alps and the deserts of Arizona. Many of the locomotives are antiques, purchased by Vanderworth from fellow collectors. Like everything else in life, Lex Luthor considers this priceless set to be expendable, and happily destroys it in pursuit of his megalomaniac experiment. How much greater will his pleasure be when he destroys a real country!

The presidential faces of Mount Rushmore stare out from a scaled-down reproduction of the Black Hills of South Dakota.

The miniature detail of the model is astonishing. Planes circle a Metropolis skyline blazing with lights, while trains arrive and depart from its central station.

Kitty can't maintain her bored expression for long once the experiment begins to work

Stanford gapes at the unfolding chemical reaction that will transform raw matter and warp the Earth's electromagnetic field.

Even in this early, unfocused experiment, the growth of the Kryptonian crystal is enough to swallow the room and split the ceiling.

SHUTTLE RESCUE

The Explorer mission marks an historic event – the first privately funded launch of a space shuttle. By piggybacking the shuttle orbiter on top of a Boeing 777 jet airliner, the craft can reach space without relying on external fuel tanks. The inaugural launch has been billed as a gala press event, and Lois Lane is one of the reporters invited to fly on board the 777. But when a mysterious electromagnetic pulse disables both the jet and the shuttle, Lois begins to think that this story could be her last.

TEST FLIGHT

According to plan, the jet is to fly to the edge of space, where the shuttle will detach and fire its fuel boosters, reaching orbit while the jet returns to Earth. Bobbie-Faye hopes that the *Explorer* will usher in an age of affordable space travel. But the electromagnetic pulse threatens to make the day a disaster.

The electromagnetic pulse that imperils the shuttle is a freak event. No one among the shocked ground crew can fix the problem in time.

The shuttle's launch was one of the biggest stories of the year; its destruction would be the biggest story of the decade. Every channel breaks into regular programming with live coverage of the crisis.

Bobbie-Faye is an aeronautics pro who has worked on the *Explorer* programme since her graduation from college. Although she's a natural saleswoman, she can't put a positive spin on the unfolding catastrophe, and panics along with everyone.

About 50 reporters, representing news channels from across the world, are trapped inside the doomed jet. The entire world is watching and hoping for a miracle. Isn't there anyone who could save them?

Superman has been doubting his role in life, but the shuttle crisis throws him right back into action. It's been five years since his last outing as a super hero, and this is one of the greatest challenges he has ever faced.

MISSION CRITICAL

A host of scientists and technicians are on hand to monitor the *Explorer* launch. If the mission succeeds, it will pave the way for super-fast transcontinental flights via low Earth orbit. But if either the jet or shuttle is destroyed, it will be the end of privately funded space travel.

SUPERMAN IS BACK

The Explorer shuttle crisis forces Superman back into his natural role as humanity's hero. From an isolated listening post high above the Earth's surface, Superman scans for signs of danger with his enhanced senses. At superspeed, he can arrive anywhere on the globe in minutes, and has soon prevented dozens of disasters. In Switzerland, he saved 12 stranded climbers from the peak of the Matterhorn. In Venice, he prevented the famous canals from flooding the city streets. Superman seems to be everywhere at once, but nowhere is he more prominent than Metropolis.

Faced with chaos, people flee for safety. Though Lois Lane, in her article *Why the World Doesn't Need Superman*, was right to champion everyday heroes, some disasters are too big for anyone but Superman.

JUST ONE MAN

Superman can travel faster than a speeding bullet, but even with his gifts he can't be everywhere at once. Superman must choose the emergencies where he can do the most good for the most people, knowing that human suffering can never be completely avoided.

Superman can lift weights above his head that not even industrial machinery could move

Combining superstrength with the power of flight, Superman can catch massive objects in mid air. Under the right conditions, Superman has carried items as heavy as ocean liners, and the upper limit of his powers remains unknown.

ROOFTOP MAYHEM

A band of armed men raid a bank vault, then sprint to the roof where a helicopter is prepared for their getaway. To delay the police arriving at the scene, one of the crooks unveils a tripod-mounted machine gun and lets loose a deadly spray of tracer bullets. Two security guards in the stairwell are gutsy enough to storm the rooftop, hoping to take down the gunner before any more officers die. When Superman arrives on the scene, will his bulletproof skin be enough to avert disaster?

YEARS AGO,

Superman made this public debut saving Lois Lane from an out-of-control helicopter. The rooftop robbers hope to escape in their own chopper, but Superman's ability to bend steel with his bare hands means they'll be going nowhere in this vehicle.

Superman's return is the biggest news of the year. The *Daily Planet* puts it on the front page, and Perry White gives Lois the job of covering the ongoing story, hoping she can land an exclusive interview.

GLOBAL PHENOMENON

The entire world, from Gotham City to Tokyo, responds to the news of Superman's appearance with a media frenzy. On high-minded news programmes and goofy entertainment chat-fests alike, everyone is talking about Superman.

KITTY'S RESCUE

It's a straightforward assignment – distract Superman at a prearranged moment, so that Lex Luthor can safely rob a museum across town. But when Kitty Kowalski sits behind the wheel of her Mustang, she doesn't realize that Lex has cut her brake lines. As the runaway vehicle swerves along busy avenues, what was supposed to be a charade quickly becomes a matter of life and death.

Before she met Lex Luthor, Kitty had pulled many scams on rich victims, following the example of her mother. Determined to prove herself to Lex, she eagerly takes on this assignment. Kitty is furious when she discovers that Lex has no regard for her safety.

RUSH HOUR

Kitty can't stop the car, and smashes her way through Metropolis traffic – creating precisely the type of scene that would draw the Man of Steel's attention. The out-of-control Mustang sideswipes other vehicles as it closes in on a packed city square. Suddenly, Superman is there, hoisting the speeding vehicle over his head. Kitty's life is saved.

Kitty's classic 1960s Ford Mustang came from the Vanderworth mansion's garage. She picked it from an array of other classic cars, feeling a connection to its sleek profile and curves.

Nerves frazzled, Kitty doesn't need to perform any theatrics to convince the Man of Steel that she survived a terrifying ordeal. By the time he has taken her to Metropolis General hospital, Lex and the others at the museum will have made a clean getaway.

Breaking News

A large crowd gathers to congratulate Superman, and one young onlooker snaps a photo on his cell phone. Tomorrow morning, the image will be splashed across the front page of the *Daily Planet*. Kitty's vehicle rescue caps a busy week for Superman, who has already stopped a robbery in Shanghai, dammed a flood in Melbourne, and saved an Egyptian village from a sandstorm.

MUSEUM HEIST

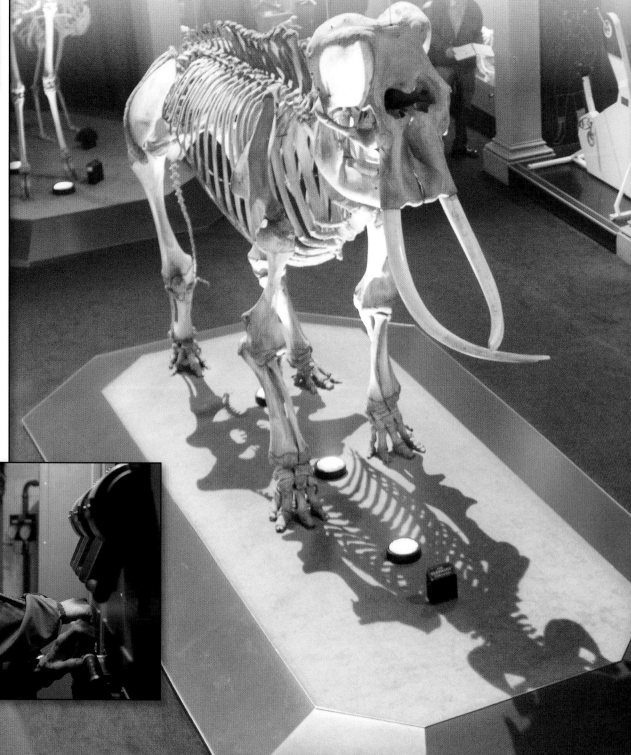

Lex Luthor once hoped that Superman would die far from Earth, fatally sickened by the kryptonite that infected the wreckage of his birth planet. When that hope was dashed, Lex moves to acquire a weapon closer to home. Reading in the *Daily Planet* that the Metropolis Museum of Natural History is hosting a rare meteorite exhibition, Lex and his henchmen plan a risky robbery. While Kitty Kowalski distracts the Man of Steel, Lex's thugs cut the museum's power. In the darkness, Lex sees one of the meteorites glow green with radioactivity under a spectral filter. It is kryptonite, and it has the power to kill Superman.

CULTURAL INSTITUTION

The Metropolis Museum of Natural History was founded with a grant from tycoon Silas Vanderworth in 1874. Only a fraction of its vast collection is on display at any time, and the museum regularly hosts traveling exhibits from across the world. Among its most popular displays are the Hall of Mammals and the Journey through Space.

Lex's thugs cut the power minutes before the museum is scheduled to close for the night. The absence of visitors allows the crooks to make a clean getaway.

COSMIC ARTIFACT

Labeled *Addis Ababa, 1978*, this green meteorite has travelled to dozens of cities as part of a mobile scientific exhibition. Like other pieces of kryptonite, the rock found itself caught up in the superluminal wake of baby Kal-El's escape pod, and landed on Earth after a journey of many light years.

Dressed as museum visitors, the criminal gang enters without attracting attention

Lex's henchmen, Grant and Brutus, carry out their boss's plan, even though both are ignorant of the power of the meteorite they are about to steal. Only Lex and Superman know what kryptonite is truly capable of.

KILLER FROM SPACE

The energy released by the explosion of Krypton's sun did more than just shatter the planet – it fused the molecules of the world's living crystals into a radioactive mass that itself burst into millions of fragments. Most kryptonite pieces are a bright green, and glow when viewed under the right lighting conditions. The radiation produced by kryptonite is harmless to humans, but wreaks havoc on Kryptonian biology. Green kryptonite attacks the same Kryptonian cells that thrive on yellow solar energy, resulting in intense pain, slowing of body functions, and within minutes, death.

This crystal is one of approximately ten that Lex pilfered from the Fortress of Solitude

Lex's scheme requires him to obtain a shard of kryptonite and an intact Kryptonian memory crystal. Using knowledge he obtained from Jor-El in the Fortress of Solitude, he will put these objects to evil ends.

Lex's henchman Stanford helped modify the shell

This metal casing, adapted from the components of a stolen military rocket launcher, will play a key role in events to come.

LOIS LANE INVESTIGATES

Though sometimes described as a scatterbrain, Lois is in fact the opposite – when she gets an idea, she can't shift her focus to anything else.

Ignoring Perry White's orders to write a puff piece about Superman, Lois zeroes in on the real story – the mysterious blackout that shut down Metropolis and triggered the *Explorer* shuttle crisis. Calls to the Department of Water and Power confirm Lois's suspicions. Like a ripple in a pond, the power outage rolled outwards from a single spot – the Vanderworth estate. Though Lois is scheduled to be the guest of honour at the Pulitzer Prize ceremony later that evening, she can't shake the feeling that the answer is just within her grasp.

Lois might be late for the ceremony, but investigations like this are what cemented her reputation as one of Metropolis's top reporters

Lois is between picking Jason up from school and driving to the award ceremony when her journalist's instincts get the better of her. Pulling up to the Vanderworth mansion, she brings Jason with her on a spur-of-the-moment investigation. Lois presses on despite the dangers, and soon finds herself caught in the web of wickedness spun by Lex Luthor.

IN THE DRAGON'S LAIR

Lex Luthor plays the gracious host, welcoming Lois and Jason to his inner sanctum where he plots to remake the face of the Earth. Confident that no one, not even Superman, can derail his plans this time, Lex taunts the woman who was once his archenemy's true love. Despite his false politeness, Lex has no intention of letting either of his captives go.

Lois knows Lex Luthor as well as anyone, and is all too aware of his capacity for cruelty and cold-blooded murder. She has come too far to back out, however, and her only concern now is to secure Jason's release.

Sending an S.O.S.

Using a fax machine as a technological stand-in for a message in a bottle, Lois transmits the cryptic code 39N71W. It is her hope that someone at the *Daily Planet* will receive the transmission, and decipher it as the latitude/longitude co-ordinates of her current location. She knows that if Lex catches on to her actions, he will kill her.

Scrawled quickly on a sheet of paper, this message is Lois's only hope

Jimmy, Richard, and Clark are worried by Lois's sudden disappearance. The three all care for Lois in their own way, and put their heads together to plan her rescue. Luckily, the fax gives clues to her whereabouts.

Lois watches Jason's breathing with concern, alert for signs of an impending asthma attack

Pulitzer winner

Lois is one of the year's recipients of the Pulitzer Prize, awarded for her story *Why the World Doesn't Need Superman*. Her colleagues are more excited about the honour than she is. Lois considers the evening's award ceremony a distraction from her investigation into the mysterious blackout.

Lois's dress was made for her by a designer specially for the Pulitzer ceremony. Created in a classic style, the gown has intricate hand-sewn beadwork. Despite its high price tag, Lois has no reservations about heading off on an adventure while wearing it.

JASON

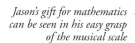

Jason's gift for mathematics can be seen in his easy grasp of the musical scale

Jason has allergies to nuts, seafood, wheat, and milk. Every morning and evening, he submits to a regimen of pills, vitamins, and eye drops. His restricted diet permits only simple foods, such as rice, tofu, steamed vegetables, and blended macrobiotic shakes.

Lois Lane never dreamed she would become a mother, flatly stating "I'd go bananas after a week" when observing her sister's noisy family. Even today, Lois can't believe the changes in her life since the arrival of her son, Jason. Born prematurely, Jason survived a stay in intensive care, but developed a host of health ailments as he grew. Lois raises Jason in the home she shares with her fiancée, Richard White, and loves her son fiercely. She now realizes that her life is all about Jason.

Jason keeps an asthma inhaler with him, but Lois and Richard always carry backups

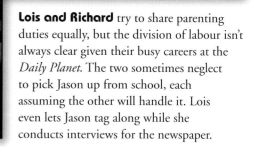

GROWING MIND

Jason is smart for his age, exhibiting a natural talent for learning, although physically he lags behind. His last report card gave him top marks in science, but poor marks in gym.

Lois and Richard try to share parenting duties equally, but the division of labour isn't always clear given their busy careers at the *Daily Planet*. The two sometimes neglect to pick Jason up from school, each assuming the other will handle it. Lois even lets Jason tag along while she conducts interviews for the newspaper.

HEART AND SOUL

Lois tries to prevent work from intruding on her home life, for reasons both personal and practical – the last time Jason touched her laptop, he accidentally erased a 4,000-word story. Jason has inherited Lois's natural stubbornness, and already shows signs of being a perfectionist. He loves the musical keyboard Lois bought him, but if he misses even a single note, he will start the piece again from the top.

Lois often brings Jason to the *Daily Planet* offices when she has nowhere else to leave him. He is a familiar sight to everyone in the bullpen, and many staffers keep toys and books in their desks to surprise him.

NEW KRYPTON

◇⠬⠤∞ ⧈⟁⠶⟊◇⠤⊤⫿⟊◇

It is a replica of the splendour of Krypton, and a mocking reminder that those glories are gone forever. New Krypton, located in the north Atlantic, took shape according to a programme inside the seed crystal. Peaks and canyons rise from the surf as the gigantic structure reveals itself. But something is wrong with this technology. Unlike the translucence of pure Kryptonian structures, its crystals are ash-coloured and sinister – a sign of the poison that lies within.

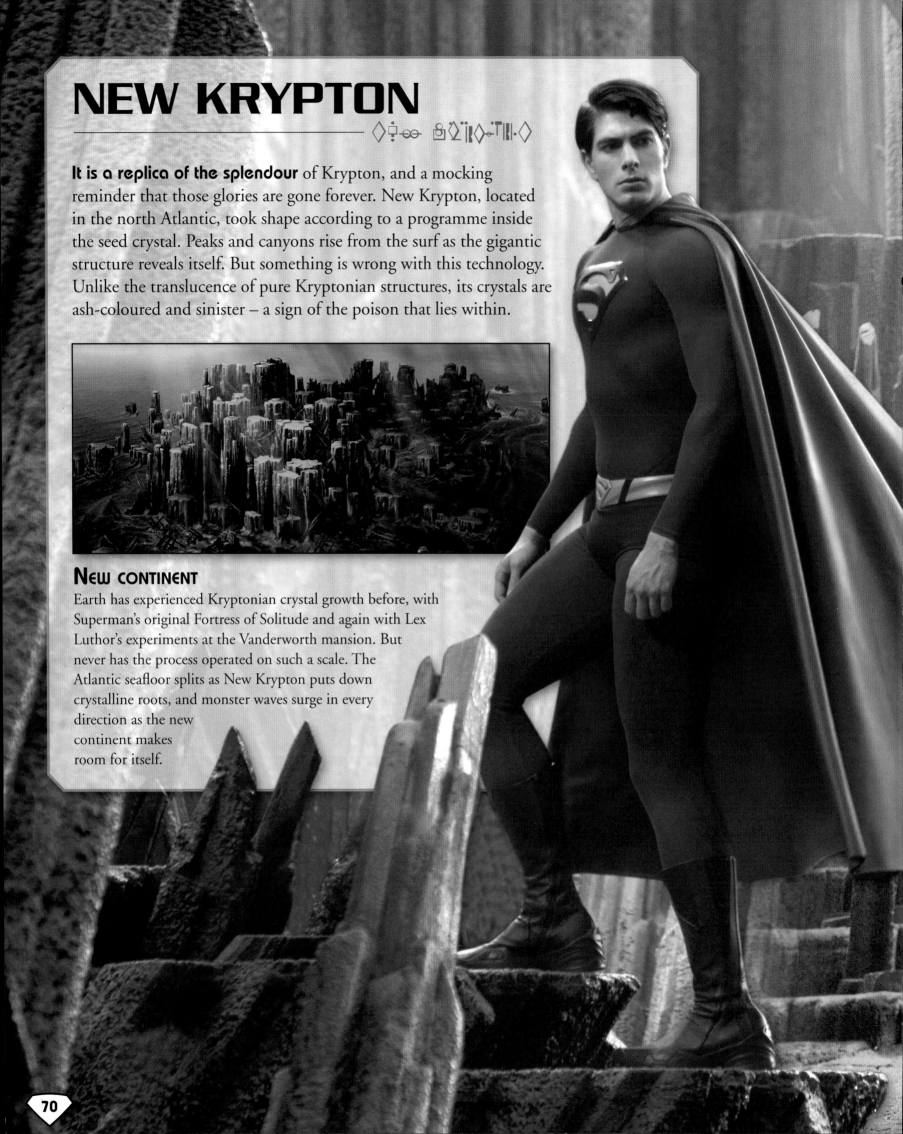

NEW CONTINENT

Earth has experienced Kryptonian crystal growth before, with Superman's original Fortress of Solitude and again with Lex Luthor's experiments at the Vanderworth mansion. But never has the process operated on such a scale. The Atlantic seafloor splits as New Krypton puts down crystalline roots, and monster waves surge in every direction as the new continent makes room for itself.

DARK CRYSTAL

New Krypton recreates its planet of origin according to an ancient blueprint, beginning with the vanished capital of Kryptonopolis. New Krypton's Valley of Elders is an empty copy of the spot where Sor-El, Kol-Ar, and Pol-Us established the laws that governed Krypton up until the time of its destruction. If the continent continues to expand, it will eventually replicate the towering face of Mount Argo, the bottomless depths of the Xan Chasm, and the polished dome of the Kryptonian Science Council. Superman walks though the alien landscape and is amazed. It is a nightmare version of the home planet he never knew. This world is shadowy, barren, and forbidding. The true Krypton was filled with light.

Superman has never set foot on this continent before, but he carries an unconscious memory of a world he never knew. A duplicate Fortress of Solitude has been erected on New Krypton, and Superman knows that the answers he seeks must be found inside.

Giant shards of crystal emerge dramatically from the floor of the structure

ACKNOWLEDGMENTS

The author would like to thank
Bryan Singer, Michael Dougherty, Dan Harris, Steve Korté,
Chris Cerasi, Marv Wolfman, Emma Rodgers, Toby Gibson,
Maureen, Squillace, Sandy Yi, Robert Perry, Jon Richards,
Alastair Dougall, and Steve Younis